SOCCER'S GREATEST MOMENTS

AUDREY STEWART

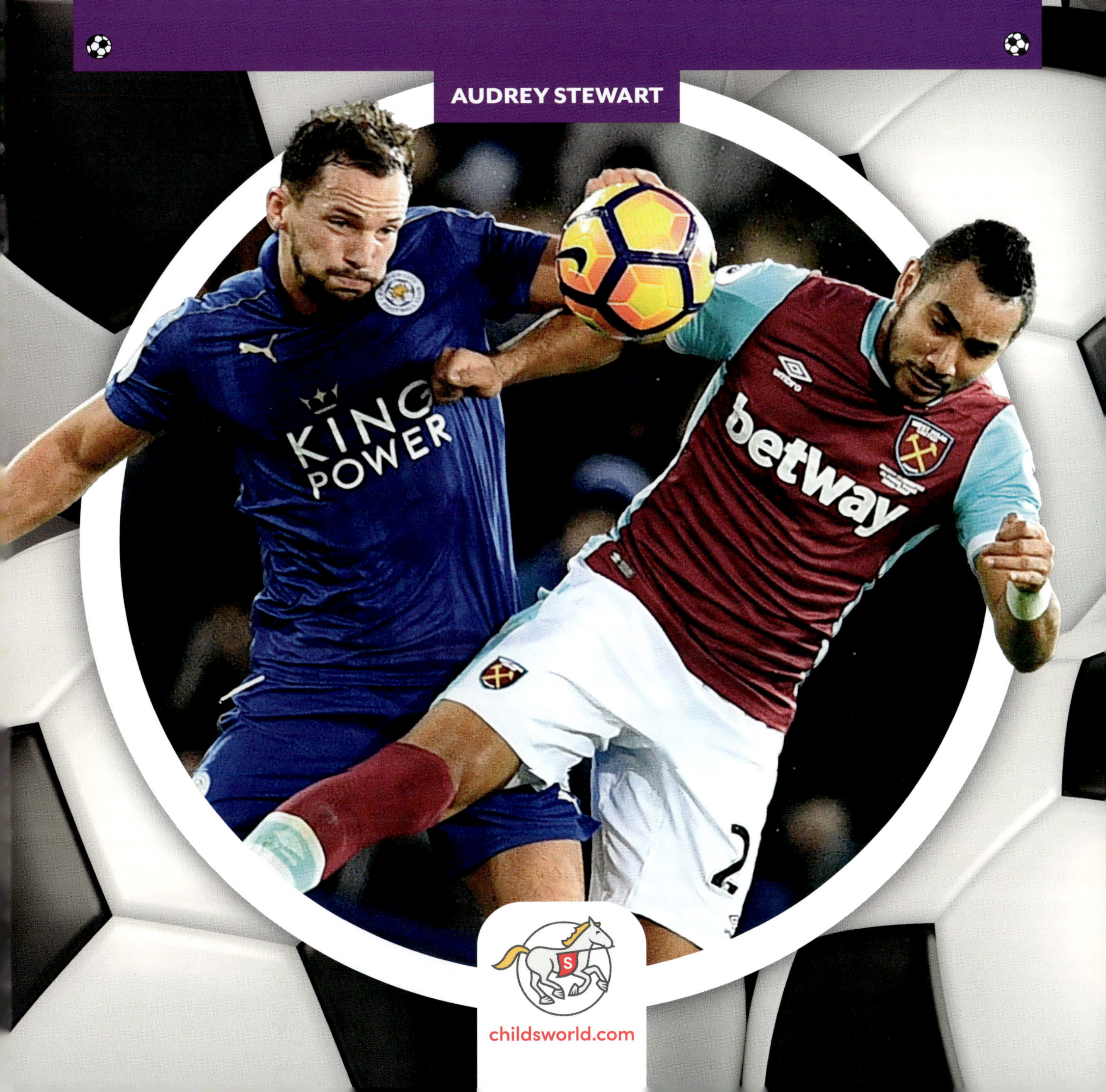

childsworld.com

Published by The Child's World®
800-599-READ • childsworld.com

Photography Credits
Cover: ©AlexeyVS/Getty Images; ©Justin Tallis/Getty Images; page 4: ©irin-k/Shutterstock; page 5: ©Martin Rickett/PA Images/Getty Images; page 6: ©Etsuo Hara/Getty Images; page 7: ©Mike Egerton/EMPICS/Getty Images; page 9: ©ullstein bild/Getty Images; ©Pascal George/Getty Images; page 10: ©Maddie Meyer/FIFA/Getty Images; page 11: ©SOPA Images/Getty Images; page 12: ©Stu Forster/Getty Images; page 13: ©Juan Mabromata/Getty Images; page 15: ©Koji Watanabe/Getty Images; page 16: ©Maja Hitij/Getty Images; page 17: ©Kirill Kudryavtsev/Getty Images; page 19: ©Picture Alliance/Getty Images; page 20: ©Alex Livesey/Danehouse/Getty Images; ©Alex Livesey/Getty Images; page 21: ©Getty Images/Getty Images; page 22: ©Phil Cole/Getty Images; page 23: ©Mirrorpix/Getty Images; page 24: ©Stu Forster/Getty Images; page 25: ©Simon M. Bruty/Getty Images; page 27: ©Adrian Dennis/Getty Images; page 28: ©Laurence Griffiths/Getty Images

ISBN Information
ISBN 9781503894297 (Reinforced Library Binding)
ISBN 9781503895263 (Portable Document Format)
ISBN 9781503896086 (Online Multi-user eBook)
ISBN 9781503896901 (Electronic Publication)

LCCN
2024942885

Printed in the United States of America

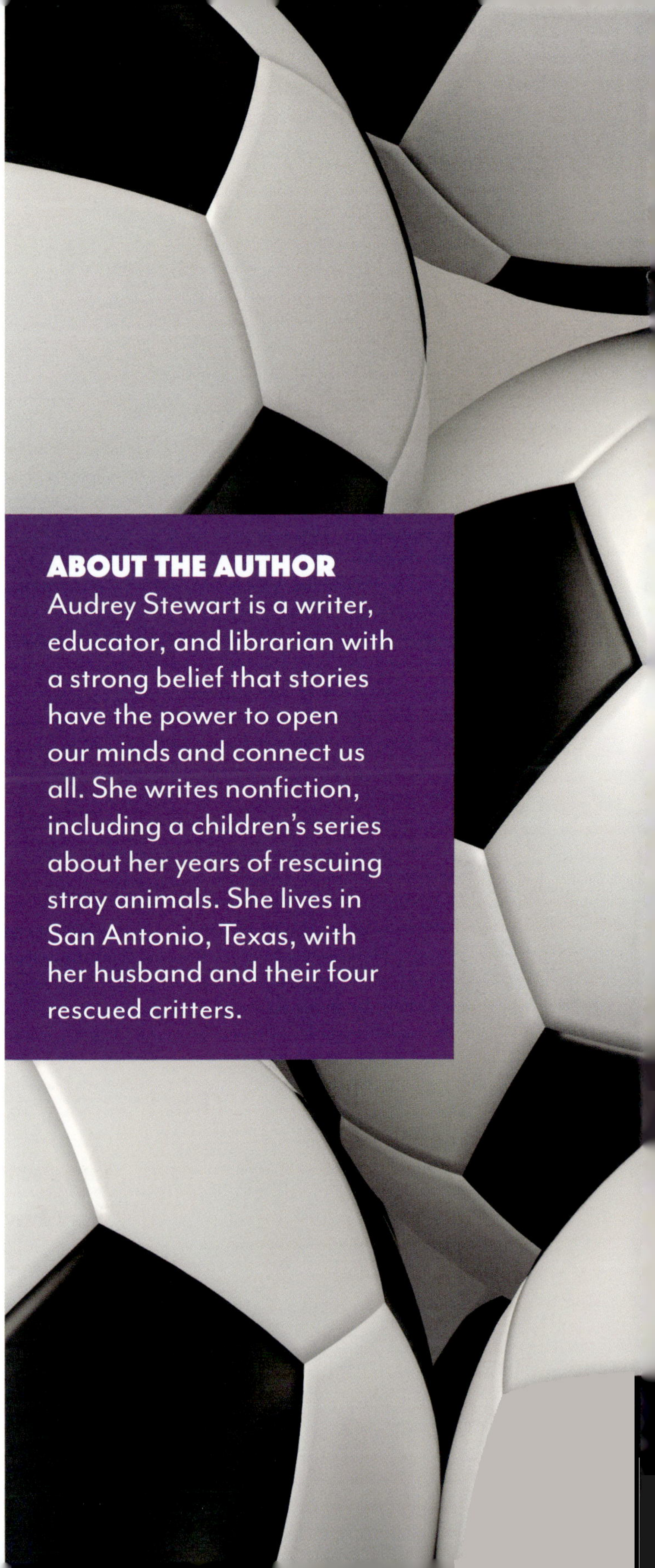

ABOUT THE AUTHOR

Audrey Stewart is a writer, educator, and librarian with a strong belief that stories have the power to open our minds and connect us all. She writes nonfiction, including a children's series about her years of rescuing stray animals. She lives in San Antonio, Texas, with her husband and their four rescued critters.

CONTENTS

CHAPTER ONE

THE BEST GAME IN THE WORLD

Soccer is one of the most popular sports in the world. It speeds by at a fast pace with no time-outs, no quarters, and no breaks. Players get a quick halftime to regroup. Fans get a few minutes to catch their breath before everyone dives in for more. Soccer is a game that requires fast decision-making and exceptional skills. Goals are often a highlight of the game. But spectacular saves are also worth watching.

Fans are left in awe when a player does something amazing or unexpected. Maybe a player scores a goal at an impossible angle. Perhaps they have amazingly fast feet and get past the most skilled defenders. Sometimes players pull off an incredible move that leaves fans in shock. Moments like these highlight the awesome skills of players and their teams.

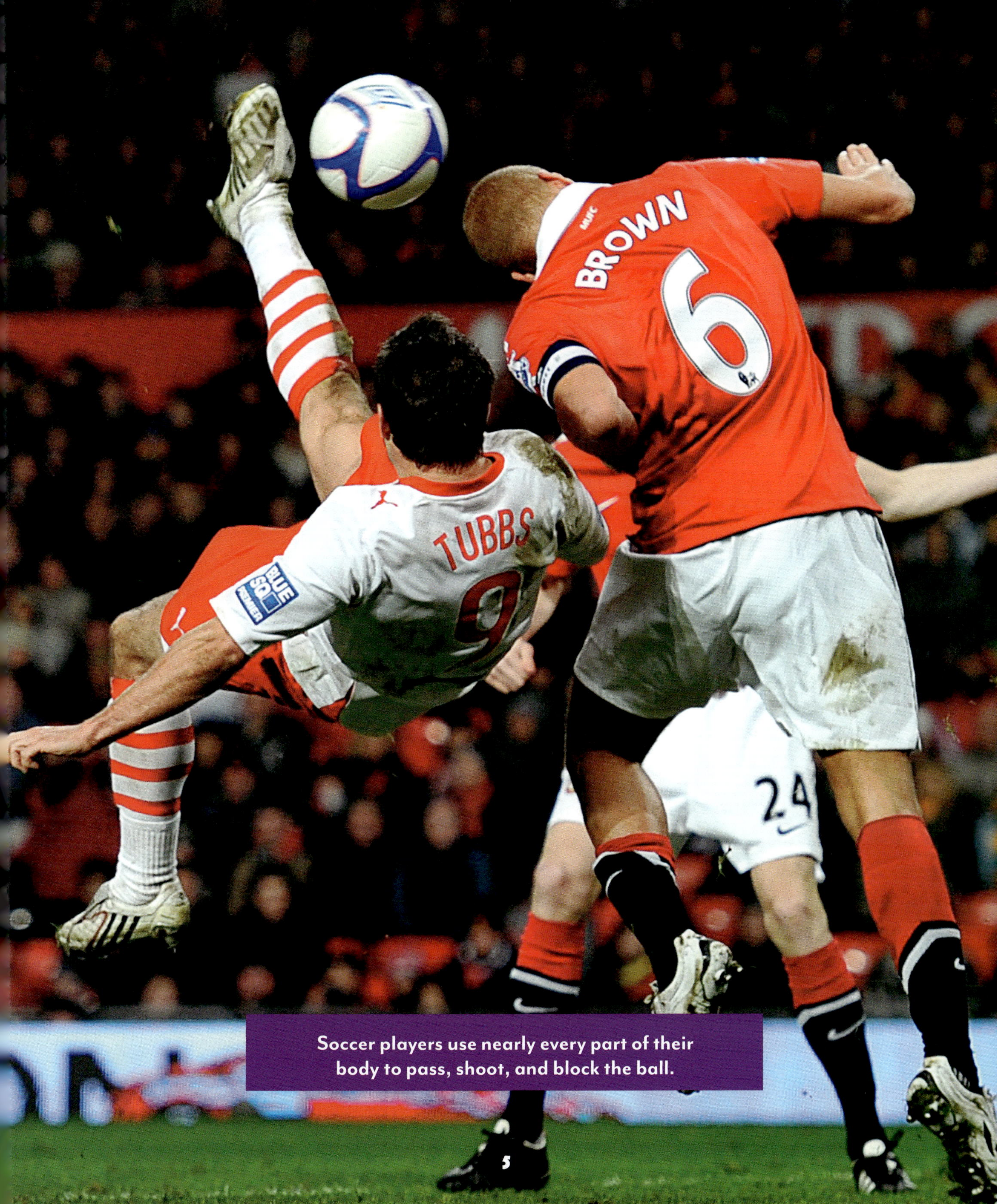

Soccer players use nearly every part of their body to pass, shoot, and block the ball.

Ronaldinho was known by the nickname *O Bruxo*, which means "The Wizard." His trick plays and quick moves made every game entertaining for fans.

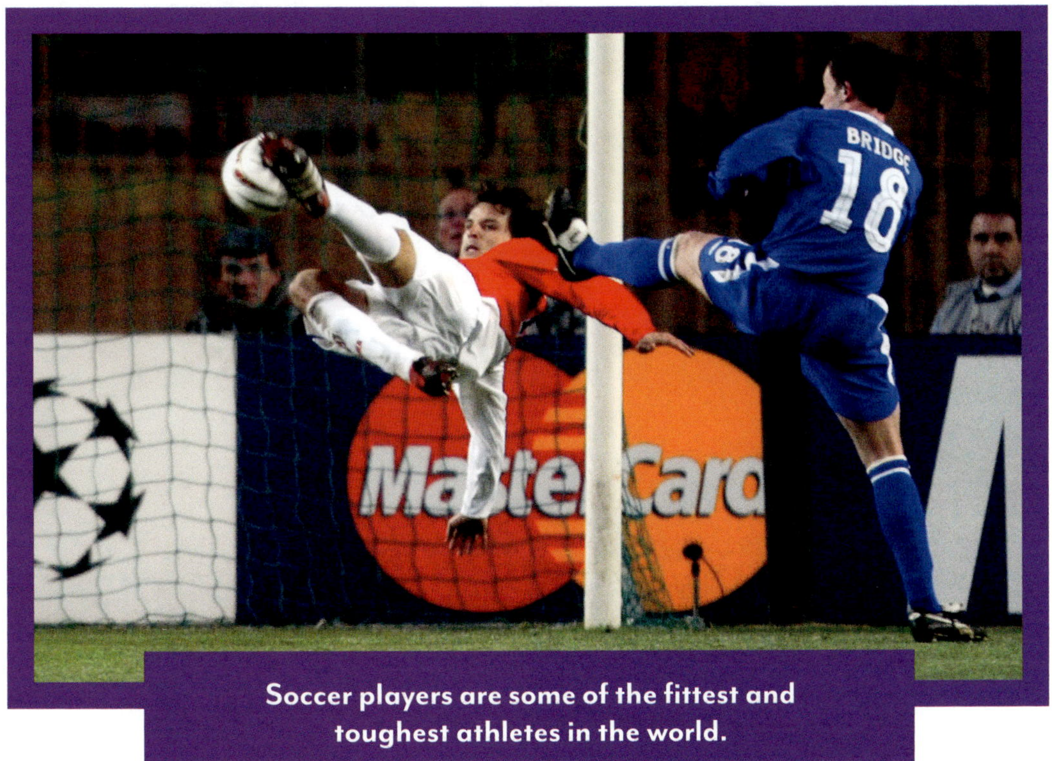

Soccer players are some of the fittest and toughest athletes in the world.

Fans love when a team comes back from losing and wins an important game. A dramatic finish to a close game can make fans talk about it for years. Big events such as the World Cup or **Champions League** finals are some examples of when great moments happen. In these moments, the stakes are high and the crowd is on the edge of their seats.

Soccer fans around the world love to talk about special and exciting moments in their favorite sport. Whether it's a star player, the effort of a team, or a big match, amazing moments get fans excited and are remembered for years to come. But what makes a split second or two in soccer so popular and memorable?

CHAPTER TWO

GREAT MOMENTS AT THE WORLD CUP

The World Cup is a tournament that happens every four years. It is always filled with great moments as top teams go head-to-head. Few teams have as many great moments as the United States Women's National Team (USWNT). In 1991, they played in the first-ever World Cup in Guangdong, China. Team USA's three star forwards were known as the Triple-Edged Sword. Carin Jennings-Gabarra, April Heinrichs, and Michelle Akers-Stahl were a force on the field. They helped make history by leading the USWNT to their first World Cup title.

The USWNT continued to make strides in the soccer world. Forward Mia Hamm played in her second World Cup tournament in 1999. Hamm scored with a **volley** only 17 minutes into the opening round against Denmark. It was the first of 17 goals the USWNT would score on their way to another first-place finish.

Brazilian legend Pelé played in four World Cup tournaments and helped his team win three of them.

HISTORY OF THE USWNT

Every memorable team has a beginning. The USWNT was formed in 1985. They played the first World Cup tournament in 1991 and appeared in the Olympic Games in 1996. It was the first time women's soccer was included in the Olympics. The 1990s was the beginning of a legendary team. The USWNT continues to change and advance not just soccer, but women's sports around the world. They have won four of the nine Women's World Cups held so far.

The USWNT has been one of the four best teams in the world since it began in 1985.

In 2019, the USWNT finished an impressive season with their fourth World Cup title. From 1999 to 2019, the team **dominated** women's sports and put women's soccer on the map. During this time, the USWNT lost only once, tied twice, and won 37 total matches. They scored 170 total goals and only allowed other teams to score 15. Team USA leads the way with the most World Cup titles for women's soccer.

The same season saw a coach's best moment. USWNT manager Jill Ellis broke the world record for most Women's World Cups won by a manager.

The 2019 World Cup also put Megan Rapinoe in the headlines as one of women's soccer's best players. Rapinoe won the **Golden Boot** for scoring six goals, the most in the tournament. She also won the **Golden Ball** as the World Cup's best player.

Megan Rapinoe started playing for the USWNT in 2006. She played in 203 games for the team and scored 63 goals.

The Men's World Cup is also packed with memorable moments. During the 1998 World Cup quarterfinals, no one could stop Netherlands forward Dennis Bergkamp. With just a few minutes remaining in a game against Argentina, a Netherlands player kicked the ball from the middle of the field. Bergkamp sprinted toward the goal and received a pass on the run. He flicked the ball around a defender and shot it into the corner of the net as the goalie came forward. The Netherlands won 2–1 to advance to the semifinals.

Dennis Bergkamp was such a skilled player that a soccer move is named for him. The "Bergkamp Turn" is a quick change in direction to keep a defender from taking the ball.

Lionel Messi is one of only six male players to appear in five World Cup tournaments. Messi and Argentina finally took home the trophy in 2022.

In 2002, two of soccer's greatest legends from Brazil met after Brazil beat Germany 2–0 to win the World Cup. Pelé, a star player from the 1958, 1962, and 1970 World Cups, greeted forward Ronaldo de Lima during the award ceremony in an **iconic** moment for fans everywhere.

In the 2022 World Cup final, Argentinian star Lionel Messi brought the team a victory in the 108th minute. He scored twice in the final, leading Argentina to a 4–2 shootout victory over France after playing to a 3–3 tie. This was Argentina's third World Cup title, but Messi's first with his national team.

CHAPTER THREE

GREAT MOMENTS AT THE OLYMPICS

The Olympic Games give players around the world a chance to compete while showing **goodwill** between many countries. The USWNT has often been the top team in this tournament as well. In 2004, Hamm and other great legends passed the torch to forward Abby Wambach. Team USA was up against Brazil for the gold medal. Wambach led the team to a victory with a **header** from a **corner kick** in the 112th minute of the gold medal match.

The 2008 Olympic Games in Beijing saw another amazing moment from USWNT player and captain Carli Lloyd in the 96th minute of the gold medal match. The US was playing Brazil, and the game was tied 0–0 in extra time. Lloyd moved past defenders and hammered the ball into the net in the final minutes of the game. The USWNT won 1–0. Four years later, the women's team won gold again, this time against Japan. This was the USWNT's fourth gold medal.

Messi is Argentina's top goal-scorer of all time. He has scored 106 goals for his country.

Also in 2008, the Olympics brought success to Argentina's men's national team. Legendary player Lionel Messi, only 21 years old, got the ball and turned quickly at an impossible angle to score in the quarterfinal game against the Netherlands. Argentina won the final match against Nigeria and took home the gold medal for the second Olympics in a row—and the world got a taste of what Messi could do with a soccer ball.

Defenders such as Magdalena Eriksson often score with headers during corner kicks when the ball sails across the front of the goal.

Four years later in London, fans were in awe of USWNT midfielder and forward Megan Rapinoe at the 2012 Olympics. Team USA was down 1–0 in the second half of the semifinal match against Canada. Rapinoe scored what is known as an Olimpico. This is a goal that goes into the net directly from a corner kick. She was the first player to score an Olimpico at the Olympics. Rapinoe's goal tied the game. USA beat Canada in extra time 4–3 and went on to defeat Japan in the gold medal match.

The 2020 Olympics in Tokyo, which took place in 2021 due to COVID-19, had many great goals. Swedish center back Magdalena Eriksson received a pass and headed the ball into the goal during a quarterfinal match against Japan. Sweden won 3 –1 and advanced to the semifinals. They lost to Canada in the final round and took home a silver medal.

SCORING WITH YOUR HEAD

Players who can time the ball just right and jump higher than their opponent might use their head to score a goal. Juventus club player Cristiano Ronaldo is good at using his head. In a match against club team Sampdoria, one of Ronaldo's teammates lofted the ball toward the penalty box. Ronaldo leaped up and appeared to hang in the air for a second before heading the ball into the corner of the goal. Ronaldo has scored more than 100 header goals!

CHAPTER FOUR

DID THAT REALLY JUST HAPPEN?

Some of the best soccer moments occur when players bend, twist, run, and dodge in incredible ways. Such skills were on full display during a 2005 match between club teams Real Madrid and Barcelona. Barcelona's Ronaldinho was up against some of the best players that season. He dazzled the crowd with his fancy footwork and produced two amazing goals. This got him a standing **ovation** from fans of both teams. Real Madrid and Barcelona are fierce **rivals**. Ronaldinho's performance was so amazing that it left even Real Madrid fans speechless.

Antonin Panenka's 1976 penalty shot is considered one of the most famous penalty kicks of all time.

When players take a penalty kick, they usually kick the ball hard to the left or right into the goal. During a 1976 championship match, Czechoslovakia faced West Germany, and Czech player Antonin Panenka was up for a penalty shot. Instead of blasting the ball, Panenka chipped the ball straight down the middle and into the goal as the goalie dove to the left. Taking this shot is now known as the Panenka Penalty.

HOW VAR CHANGED THE GAME

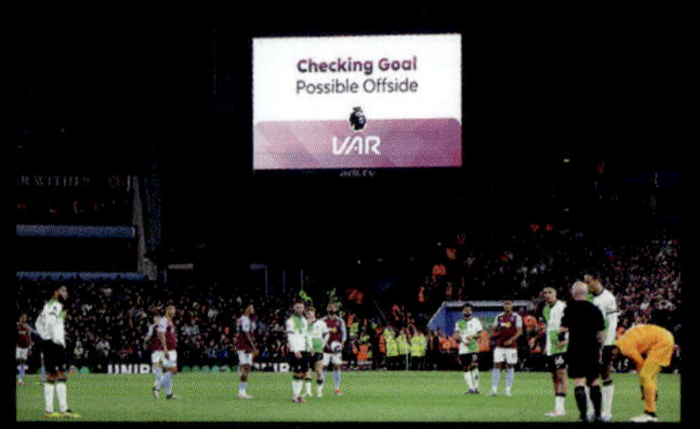

FIFA introduced Video Assisted Referee (VAR) in 2012, but it was not used widely until 2017. It has changed the game of soccer in many ways. This new technology allows referees to rewatch a questionable foul or **offside** call. Using VAR allows referees to change or reverse a call. Some experts believe it has reduced the number of fouls and offside calls for all teams. But many players feel VAR has resulted in a slower game with more stoppage time. And if VAR technology had existed earlier, some big moments, including Maradona's handball goal, wouldn't have existed!

Any player who can score with a bicycle kick deserves to be recognized. A bicycle kick is when a player does a backward somersault with their legs in the air. The pedal motion propels the ball. In 2011, Manchester United player Wayne Rooney scored a bicycle kick goal against rival team Manchester City. Rooney scored with just 12 minutes left in the game, and Manchester United won the match.

Wayne Rooney's bicycle kick goal against Manchester City is considered the best goal of all time between the two teams.

Maradona's "Hand of God" goal would have probably been called back if VAR had existed in 1986.

The most iconic moment in soccer is the Hand of God. During the 1986 World Cup, Argentina played England in the quarterfinal match. Diego Maradona used his hand to score the goal. VAR didn't exist at the time, so officials could not review the play. Conversations about the goal and whether it should have been allowed continue to this day. Maradona admitted that the ball touched his hand. He claimed the win was payback from Argentina losing to the United Kingdom in the Falklands War four years earlier.

CHAPTER FIVE

MAKING HISTORY

Soccer teams work hard to win it all. When a team wins a league championship, a national title, and an international title in the same season, it is known as a treble. An example is the English Premier League, the FA Cup, and the Champions League. These competitions involve the best teams from the current season. Coming in first place for all three is quite a defining moment for a team. Only two teams have won the Premier League treble in the history of **professional** soccer in England. In 1999, David Beckham and Manchester United became the first to accomplish this rare feat.

David Beckham signed his first contract with Manchester United at just 16 years old. He is one of England's best-known players.

Since the 1998–1999 season, only Manchester United's rival, Manchester City, has won the Premier League treble.

The treble was a highlight in Beckham's career with Manchester United. He was voted Young Player of the Year for the 1996–1997 season in just his third year as a professional. One magical moment came in the semifinal round of the Champions League. Manchester United was down 2–0 in the first 11 minutes. It wasn't looking good for them. Captain Roy Keane stepped in and scored a header off Beckham's corner kick to rally the team. The team scored again to tie the match and pulled ahead in the closing minutes to win the match.

Erling Haaland also plays for his home country of Norway. He once scored nine goals in a single match.

In the 2003–2004 season, the English team Arsenal made history. Called the Invincibles, the team went undefeated for 38 league games. Arsenal is the only team to ever finish a 38-match season undefeated. Their winning streak continued to a record of 49 matches. In total, they won 26 matches, had 12 ties, and suffered no defeats.

In November 2023, Erling Haaland made history in English football. In a match against Liverpool, Haaland scored his 50th Premier League goal. This feat made him the quickest player to reach 50 or more goals in the league.

RONALDINHO'S MEMORABLE SKILLS

Brazilian player Ronaldinho Gaúcho is one of football's greatest players. He was always entertaining when he was on the field. His speed, strength, and style of play captivated fans from all over the world. Ronaldinho's ability to score and play in many different positions always kept his opponent guessing. He is best known for his use of tricks and fakes to create goal-scoring opportunities.

CHAPTER SIX

THE UNEXPECTED

Sometimes great moments surprise fans—for better or for worse. Sometimes teams that aren't expected to win do just that. And teams that are sure to win sometimes lose. One of the greatest comebacks in a European Cup final game was between Liverpool and Milan in 2005. Liverpool hadn't played in the finals in more than 20 years. Milan was the dominant team. At halftime, Liverpool was losing 3–0. Liverpool scored three goals in the second half. The match went into extra time, and Liverpool won in a **shoot-out**. It was their first European Cup win since 1984.

One of the greatest stories in soccer is that of Leicester City Football Club's comeback in the 2015–2016 season. It was a classic story of an underdog team working hard to win it all. The previous season, Leicester City finished in 14th place. The odds were not in their favor. But thanks to the team's lineup and a new style of play, Leicester City won the Premier League in 2016.

Teams that do not have much of a chance of winning are known as underdogs. Leicester City had never finished first in the Premier League before 2016.

David Seaman had 137 clean sheets during his time with Arsenal. A clean sheet means that a goalie did not allow the other team to score any goals during a game.

Goalies are the last line of defense for a team. Many of soccer's most memorable moments are incredible stops, blocks, and dives in the goal. Arsenal legend David Seaman is one amazing goalkeeper. He stopped Sheffield United's Paul Peschisolido from scoring a brilliant goal in a 2003 tournament semifinal game. Only a few minutes were left on the clock. Sheffield United booted a corner kick to the penalty box. Peschisolido took the shot, and it looked like it was going in. Seaman spread his fingers wide to push the ball out and away as he fell to the ground. Seaman's save was described as "the claw."

From close saves to impossible goals, soccer is a game of seconds and inches. Legends are born when the unexpected happens on the field. These moments keep fans coming back for more.

GLOSSARY

Champions League (CHAM-pee-uns LEEG) a soccer competition held each year between the best teams from Europe

corner kick (KOR-nur KIK) a kick taken from the corner of the defending team's end of the field after the defending team kicks the ball over their own goal line

dominated (DOM-uh-nay-tud) was the best in a particular area

FIFA (FEE-fah) FIFA, short for Fédération Internationale de Football Association, is the group that oversees international soccer

Golden Ball (GOL-dun BALL) a trophy awarded to the best player in a FIFA tournament such as the World Cup

Golden Boot (GOL-dun BOOT) a trophy awarded to the top goal-scorer in a FIFA tournament such as the World Cup

goodwill (good-WILL) an attitude of kindness and cooperation between people

header (HED-dur) a shot or pass in soccer made with the head

iconic (eye-KON-ik) relating to a person or event that is widely recognized by many people

offside (off-SIDE) a foul in soccer called when the attacking player is past the last defender from the other team

ovation (oh-VAY-shun) a show of support with enthusiastic clapping

professional (pro-FESH-uh-nul) taking part in a sport for money

rivals (RY-vals) two teams or individuals competing for the same goal

shoot-out (SHOOT-owt) a tie-breaker that involves each team taking penalty kicks

volley (VOL-lee) to strike the ball before it touches the ground

FAST FACTS

- The FIFA World Cup is one of the largest sporting events in the world. It is held every four years.
- The fastest goal in soccer history was scored by Scottish player Gavin Stokes. He scored a goal just 2.1 seconds into the game.
- Women's soccer became an Olympic sport in 1996, and Team USA won gold.
- Only five countries have won the Women's World Cup: the United States, Spain, Japan, Germany, and Norway.

ONE STRIDE FURTHER

- What did you learn about great soccer moments from reading this book? Describe a great moment in soccer or another sport.
- Ask your friends and family if they know about any great moments in sports. Make a list and see if any great moments are mentioned more than once.
- Choose one of the moments from the list and draw a picture to capture the moment.
- What do you think makes a great moment in sports?

FIND OUT MORE

IN THE LIBRARY

Folgar, Carlos and Deborah Crisfield. *The Everything Kids' Soccer Book: Rules, Techniques, and More about Your Favorite Sport!* New York, NY: Adams Media, 2021.

Vegara, Maria Isabel Sánchez. *Leo Messi*. London, England: Frances Lincoln Children's Books, 2023.

Walters, Meg. *World Cup Women: Megan, Alex, and the Team USA Soccer Champs*. New York, NY: Sky Pony, 2019.

ON THE WEB

Visit our website for links about great moments in soccer:
childsworld.com/links

Note to Parents, Caregivers, Teachers, and Librarians: We routinely verify our web links to make sure they are safe and active sites. So encourage your readers to check them out!

INDEX